I0648760

Hamish Hendry

Burns from Heaven

With Some other Poems

Hamish Hendry

Burns from Heaven
With Some other Poems

ISBN/EAN: 9783744711432

Printed in Europe, USA, Canada, Australia, Japan

Cover: Foto ©Thomas Meinert / pixelio.de

More available books at **www.hansebooks.com**

BURNS

FROM

HEAVEN

WITH·SOME·OTHER POEMS

BY

HAMISH

❋HENDRY❋

ANNO 1897

GLASGOW·DAVID·BRYCE·&·SON

DY.C

To

Three Good Women

𝔐other: 𝔖ister: 𝔚ife:

This book is gratefully

Dedicated

CONTENTS

BURNS FROM HEAVEN

WHA says that Robbie Burns is deid?
Wha says he lies below the weed,
A pickle stoor, baith heart an' heid,
    This hunner year?
Deil blast the loons! but they hae lee'd,
    For Robin's here!

Here whare the Cluden, 'neath the mune,
Gangs happin' to the same auld tune;
Whare hoolets to the midnicht win'
    Mak' eerie mane;
Here whare I focht wi' sangs an' sin
    In days lang gane.

B

For Heaven is guid, but Scotland's best!
Sae when they gie the herps a rest
I tak' a frien'ly, quiet request
        To Peter Doot;
An' he, guid man, swears at the hest,—
        But lets me oot!

Behint me clinks the gowden yett;
An' faith! the psalms I sune forget
As doon the road I skelp sherp-set,
        Past star an' planet,
Wi' thochts o' hame that bizz red-het
        Aneath my bannet!

An' when I stap oot ower the cluds,—
There's Scotland yet! The birlin' fluds;
The broomy braes; the whusslin' wuds;
        Gowans the same!
God! but my heart starts aff in thuds,
        To ken I'm hame!

10

Saftly I daunder up an' doon
By Ayr an' Nith, by Embro' toon,
A licht-fit, liltin', hame-daft loon!
        Ilk stream, ilk tree,
The mavis' sang, the cushie's croon,
        Brings joy to me!

Yet Scotland's changed since first I kent it;
The Gospel-faulds hae been augmentit;
The hypocrites hae a' repentit,
        An' quat their quirks;
The auld black creeds hae been white-pentit
        In a' the kirks!

Nae mair frae pupits yerks a yell
O' God's damnation fierce an' fell;
A saft an' couthie tale they tell,
        An' tell it quick;
They've sell't the guid auld brunstane Hell,
        An' pensioned Nick!

A land o' saunts it would appear!
Stories o' death their daily cheer;
Whare ilk ane sits beside the Brier
        Plantit by Ian;
Whare a' men drap the mild saut tear
        Beloved in Zion.

Nae lad plays pliskie wi' a lass;
Nae fule tak's hame a stotterin' glass;
Nae stirk gangs furth a college-ass,—
        Baalam's the mate o't;
The Lord kens hoo it comes to pass,
        But that's the gate o't.

An' as for Bards,—they're scarce as brose!
But kailyaird gents, stript to the hose,
Keep dibble-dibblin' at the prose
        For English stots;
An' Lun'on toon pays through the nose
        In gowden groats!

12

Guid faith! I ken na wha can fash
To read sic screeds o' auld wives' clash;
The teary-weary, cantin' hash
    Is nocht but haivers;
An' yet the birkies, prood an' gash,
    Brag o' their clavers!

Leeze me on tales o' deils an' drink;
On canty sangs that jouk an' jink
Wi' rowth o' luve, wi' rowth o' clink!
    But bards an' bottle,
Ballant an' sang, hae taen a kink
    O' d——d teetotal!

As for mysel', I'm saunt or hog
In this man's praise, or that man's prog;
My very statues glower incog.,
    For jaw an' nose is
As like this common, rough phizog
    As I'm like Moses!

The critic-craws still bigg their hame
'Mong Robin's fauts, on Robin's fame;
Ilk rag-tag rhyme that bears his name
    Is brocht their beak in;
An' a' his bits o' sin an' shame
    Gang to the theekin'.

Deil roast sic craws an' a' their cawin'!
Their blame is stale, their praise is stawin';
When Robin drank he paid his lawin',
    Sure that's weel kenned;
When Robin fell he mourned his faain',—
    So there's an end!

Faith! if the truth maun be confest,
Auld Scotland's guid, but Heaven is best;
A body's frien's there stand the test
    Withouten sham;
Guid fellows a' at crack the jest,
    An' pass the dram.

14

Shakespeare, the king o' a' the core;
Byron, a deil to start a splore;
Shelley, whase gowden lilts galore
    Keeps a' herps waitin';
Coleridge, whiles seraph,—whiles a bore,
    Like Milton's Latin!

But Scott's the wale o' men for me,
Wi' pawkie Allan at his knee,
An' gleg James Hogg, wha thraws a wee
    At burly Kit;
An' Louis,—blythe of late cam' he,—
    A' shanks an' wit.

Wi' siclike frien's Scots saunts come sair;
Sae back to Scotland I'll nae mair;
For after Heaven I canna bear
    Sic godly folk;
Then fareweel! daylicht's in the air,
    An' there's the cock!

A CITY PASTORAL

Look down, white summer moon, look down,
  From out thy place of starry quiet;
See where the red lights o' the town
  Throb through the midnight riot.

There, on the still slope of the night,
  Thy stars about thee touched with pallor,
How looks it from that deep calm height,
  This coil of human squalor?

16

Thy soft white radiance slants the street,
  Sifts down these dark unhappy places;
Shines, through the gas-glare and the heat,
  On haggard sin-grimed faces.

Say, since thy climbing slackens where
  Orion may not follow after,—
Say, dost thou hear strike on the air
  Shrieks, ravelled up with laughter?

Oh, summer moon, how looks it then,
  Seen from these dusk-soft dreamy levels?
Doth it not cross thy calm that men
  Reel, maddened into devils?

Nay: though a woman's shriek yet shrills
  In stifled echoes down this alley,
Thy white flame tops the twilight hills
  High o'er a northern valley.

Sure it is peace to look upon
    Thy slow light sloping down the passes;
Gleam of thy going on grey stone,
    With shimmer on wet grasses.

Thy presence keeps the quiet sky;
    Thy glimmered light goes on the meadows,
Where drowsy sheep together lie
    Silent, beside their shadows.

So while the valley seems to swim
    Spacious beneath thy loosened splendour,
There spreads a sound of evening hymn;
    Treble, and clear, and tender

With children's voices; and the song
    Is that old Galilean story
Which Bethlem's shepherds heard the throng
    Chant in the sudden glory.

" Peace and Goodwill o'er all the earth,"
   Along the moonlit slope is drifted
By voices, at a cottar's hearth
   On northern hills, uplifted.

And thou art *here,* O summer moon,
   Radiant above this city's riot!
Thou who hast heard the children's tune
   Drift on that valley's quiet.

PEACE

THE red sun passes into sight,
  In lateness of this autumn morn;
The long street takes its slanted light
  In settled stillness, sabbath-born:
    For toiling men from toiling cease,
    And the great city lies in peace.

The house-roofs glisten, white with rime;
  The house-fires lift their shafted smoke;
From far there comes the belfry's chime
  .That starts the week-day hammer-stroke:
    But toiling men from toiling cease,
    And the far-chiming falls on peace.

Yon throstle pipes its prison-song
  In cadenced clearness full and sweet;
In bursts of singing loud and long
  It stirs the echo of the street:
      When toiling men from toiling cease,
      A bird's note deepeneth the peace.

Sing out, brave bird, behind thy bar!
  So will I add a note to thine:
Our mated music shall not mar
  The sacred day; nor yours nor mine:
      When toiling men from toiling cease,
      We singers claim the hours of peace.

The mellow sunlight brings to thee
  Remembrance of red autumn woods;
My thought, unburdened, brings to me
  Home,—and its hallowed neighbourhoods:
      Where fisher-folk from toiling cease,
      And sea-horizons spread their peace.

I see the white church on the shore;
  The dawn, red-dripping on the waves;
The night-mist rising, chill and hoar,
  Above the hamlet's lonely graves:
    The toiling tides that never cease;
    The rime-white mounds in rankéd peace.

My old home by the Nor'land Sea!
  Thy love within my heart is set,
Thy beauty lingers long with me;
  I scorned thee once; I love thee yet:
    When toiling men from toiling cease,
    Their hearts turn home for perfect peace.

SUN-TAN

NOON: with the stark sun throbbing in a blaze
Of molten light; low hills aswim with haze;
Horizon-clouds dusk-soft i' the sullen heat;
A dim, moist land, rank-green to where the wheat
Pours yellow torrent on the slope; with line
Of sky-gapped firs sombre against the shine.
No stir of life, save where yon reaper reaps
Solitary; soundless his white steel leaps
In the bog-grass; patient, with plash of foot
Monotonous he goes.   The birds are mute;
Yet unto me,—prone in the matted grass,
Heedless of aught the hot hour brings to pass,—
Cometh a drift of song; a wayward note,
Wherewith the Singer seems to dance and float:—

23

I follow the World with frolic-kiss,—
   Kiss of a laughing Lover;
I go where I may, woo whom I wis:
Sure never merrier Life than this
   Can Earth or Air discover.

I was a page in Titania's train,
   Loved of the Queen and petted;
I led the Revels in moonlit lane
Where shadows mixed: but I grew fain
   Of lustier Life, and fretted.

Wanton, in sooth, was the Fay Queen's court;
   Goodly the smooth green spaces;
Gaily we rade in roystering sort:
Yet I grew fain of winsomer Sport,
   Bedight in blyther graces.

It was in the Hour when stars went wan,
   And Fairies home had ridden;
When dewy Silence lay on the lawn
Where the dance had stirred,—I waited the Dawn
   Deep in May-blossom hidden.

For I had woven of wayward whim
   A fairy web of treason;
And thus, when the Hour sent life abrim
I waited the strong, sweet will of Him
   Who rules the brighter season.

A little grey Wind slipped by, and shook
   The blossoms all awhisper;
The Dark crept softly from nook to nook;
The Dawn swept in and smote the brook
   Whitelier yet, and crisper.

All hushed in the white May-bloom I lay,
    A dusk Thing chilled and chidden,
With thought that I was a foolish Fay,—
When soft! the Sun's voice, stirring the spray,
    Atween the leaves was thridden.

Aslant and warm was the message sent:—
    " Thou shalt be mine hereafter;
The noontide blue it shall be thy Tent;
Thy name Sun-Tan";—here the King's voice went
    In ripples of brown laughter.

I gat me out from the May-flower's mid,
    Brisk with a morning valour;
Aswing on the spray, with winking lid,
I felt me free of the Day, and rid
    Of creeping moon-bred pallor;

Forever free of the Day: to dance
  While mellow tunes are pipen;
To weave the fields in a golden trance;
And between the vines to glint askance
  When glossy juices ripen.

To follow the World with frolic-kiss,—
  Kiss of a laughing Lover;
To go where I may, woo whom I wis:
Sure never merrier Life than this
  Can Earth or Air discover.

I love the lovers of open Sky!
  Oh! many they, and motley!
All easy friends of an honest eye,
Who toss me greeting as I go by,
  Racing the South Wind hotly:

27

The Gipsy tenting beneath the bough
  Low-bent with hazel cluster;
The Reaper at rest with shaded brow;
The Sailor guiding a lazy prow
  O'er seas of windless lustre;

And straying Lovers 'tween trellised bines,
  Bright as they go together;
With swaying Dancers beneath hot vines;
With Shepherd Lad who idly twines
  A bluebell with the heather.

The Children love me; my way is meek
  With young brows whitely simple;
And many a tender noontide freak
I set in the smooth of a rosy cheek,
  With glowing dance and dimple.

The wrinkled Elders I woo; to win
  Smiles of a welcome comer;
In leafy haunt from the household din
We lurk together; till blood erst thin
  Throbs with an ancient Summer.

Oh! fairest thing is the Human Face,
  Sad though it be, or merry;
And a winsome joy for me to trace
A touch of shining, to add a grace
  Soft as a sun-ripe berry.

To follow the World with frolic-kiss —
  Kiss of a laughing Lover;
To go where I may, woo whom I wis
Sure never merrier Life than this
  Can Earth or Air discover

BEYOND LOCHABER

THE sun made merry with the sea;
  In smile and laugh they sped the jest;
And we went sailing, sailing free,
  Among the islands of the west:
Light on our hearts lay human ills,
As blue haze on the summer hills.

We were a varied, jocund crew,
  Our many lives a tangled web;
Our friendships in the sunshine grew,
  Our flowing laughter knew no ebb:
Whate'er of good our lives might lack,
That day we left a sunny track.

We scare the lonely island-peace
  With breezy jesting leeward blown;
Of care our thought has sweet surcease,—
  The wide horizon is our own:
Afar the Coolins dimly show
In the thick sunshine's throbbing glow.

A hamlet on our larboard lies
  Within the shadow of a hill;
In gleams of white all dreamy-wise
  It takes the sunshine warm and still:
The blue smoke, rising, thinly stirs
Against the blackness of the firs.

But see! the captain's silent beck,—
  Our flag dips half-way down the mast;
A sudden hush creeps o'er the deck,
  While slowly, slowly is borne past
A burden black; no word is said;—
We stand in presence of the dead.

31

A boat, with harsh and measured oar,
  Comes slowly through the summer sea;
A wail floats wildly from the shore,
  And passes seaward waveringly:
The sunny peace is swiftly rent
From flashing sea to firmament.

All hushfully we gather round;
  The coffined dead goes down the side
With reverend hands; no speech, no sound,
  Save the long wail that wavers wide:
God! see there, twinkling in the sun,—
"*Flora MacKenzie, twenty-one!*"

And that is all: The steamship throbs,
  The boat goes on the whitened waves;
While strong men here choke down their sobs,
  And see the grass on far-off graves,
Slow dies the creaking of the oar,
Slow dies the wail along the shore.

The sun made merry with the sea,
　In smile and laugh they sped the jest;
While we went sailing, sailing free,
　Among the islands of the west:
But on our hearts lay human ills,
As thunder-clouds on summer hills.

FUNERAL OF THOMAS CARLYLE

ECCLEFECHAN, 10th Feby., 1881

SLOW tolls the bell beneath the sombre sky;
   Slow spreads the hush along the still grey light:
They bring him dead who shall not surely die,—
   They bring him home across the wintry white,—
      Here where the poor folks wait
      Silent, beside the gate.

This narrow gateway in the churchyard wall;
   These simple village-folk to bow the head;
The land made fair with snow; and over all
   A low grey cloud: so bring they home the dead.
      Drear as it thus befell,
      He would have deemed it well.

34

Stand hushed, ye kindly folk, and let him pass;
  Long hath he toiled who comes to take his peace.
The man was great; yet little men, alas!
  Shall mock his height, soon as these dead-bells
    cease.
        But he shall safely in
        Beside his silent kin.

Slow tolls the bell beneath the sombre sky;
  Slow comes the hearse against the still grey light:
They bring him dead who shall not surely die,—
  They bring him home when all the land is white,—
        Here where the sad folk wait
        Silent, beside the gate.

CHRISTMAS ON THE FRONTIER

TIE up these bells; blow out these lights;
　Let cease this mock of mumbled prayer;
Christ walks the Lands; from bastioned heights
　The cry He hears is,—" Who goes there?"

From frontier unto frontier fares
　The Man of Peace; His face is pale;
His feet are pierced; sad heart He bears
　From sentry unto sentry's hail.

He sees red watch-fires on the snows;
　Massed legions where the moon flits white;
Hears, where the muffled tumbril goes,
　Fierce cry of wolves across the night.

Christ finds no home; no place has He
　Save in the deaf priest's mumbled prayer;
Nations, else sundered, grim agree
　To ring Him challenge,—" Who goes there?"

THE BEADLE'S LAMENT

NAE mair, auld Sabbath Book, nae mair
Shall we twa tak' the poopit stair;
Aneth my arm wi' decent care
  Ye've traivelled lang;
But noo, like bauchles past repair,
  We twa maun gang.

For yon sleek Herd, wi' face o' whey,
Wha cam' last Spring frae yont Glenspey,
Has set his will, has wrocht his wey,
  Wi' laird and cottar;
Till e'en the Session are as cley,
  And he the pottar!

He's turned the auld kirk upside-doon;
Pentit the wa's blue, green, and broon;
The book-brod, tossled roun' and roun',
　　　　Glowers wi' red plush on't;
And in the pews ilk glaiket loon
　　　　Cocks whare he's cushon'd!

The douce precentor, Dauvit Parks,
Nae mair in his bit boxie barks;
An organ, stuffed wi' water-warks,
　　　　Mak's a' lugs dirl:
And twa-three lads in lang white sarks
　　　　Start aff the skirl.

A braw new Bible has been bocht,—
Revised, to clink wi' Modern Thocht;
A braw new beadle has been socht,
　　　　Soople and snod;
And this new Herd, himsel' has wrocht
　　　　A braw new God!

A God wha wadna fricht the craws;
A God wha never lifts the taws;
Wha never heard o' Moses' laws,
        On stane or paper;
A kind o' thowless Great First Cause,
        Skinklin' thro' vapour.

As for the Bible, if you please,
He thinks it's true,—in twa degrees;
Some pairt is chalk, some pairt is cheese;
        But he'll engage
To riddle oot the biggest lees
        Frae ilka page!

The Fall, he thinks, is nocht but fable;
Adam ne'er delved, nor killed was Abel;
Men never built the Tower of Babel;
        Nor lenched an Ark;
While auld Methuselah's birthday-table
        Clean jumps the mark!

No that he says sic things straucht oot;
Lord! he's as sly's Loch Leven troot;
But here wi' Science, there wi' Doot
      He crams his sermons;
Thrawin' the plainest text aboot
      To please the Germans.

The auld blue Hell he thinks a haiver;
The auld black Deil a kintry claver;
And what is Sin, but saut to savour
      Mankind's wersh luggies?
While Saunts, if ye'd believe the shaver,
      Are kirk-gaun puggies!

The Lord have mercy on sic teachin'
And on the kirk that tholes sic speech in;
A heathen-man, wi' heathen screechin',
      Were less to blame;
Satan himsel' would damn sic preachin'
      For very shame!

Oh! for the days when sinners shook
Aneth the true Herd's righteous crook;
When men were telt that this auld Book
      Is God's ain word;
When texts were stanes waled frae the brook,
      And prayer a sword.

Four ministers I've seen ta'en ower
To yon kirkyaird; and a' the four
Were men o' prayer, were men o' power,
      In kirk and session;
Preachers wha nailed ye wi' a glower
      To your transgression.

Oh! for sic men o' godly zeal;
Men wha could grab ye, head and heel,
And slype ye to the Muckle Deil,
      Withoot a qualm;
The sinner thro' the reek micht squeal,—
      They sang a psalm!

Stout Herds were they, and steeve their creed;
But this Chiel drones a wee bit screed,
In which God's will, and what Christ dreed,
      Are things to guess on;
Yammers for our Eternal need
      A bairn's schule-lesson.

A wee schule-lesson dull and dowff;
Scribbled atween twa games at gowff;
For at the tee he mak's his howff
      Baith syne and sune:—
But wha cares for a beadle's bowff
      Wha's day is dune.

My day is dune; and richt or wrang
The thocht comes like a waefu' sang;
This Book and me, we've traivelled lang
      The poopit stair;
But that's a gate we twa shall gang
      Nae mair, nae mair!

BLOW, NORTH WIND, BLOW

BLOW, north wind, blow! from shores where white
    seas thunder
  Round shining snows; blow strong, wild wind,
    blow free;
Let thy shrill bugles shriek, as bergs that sunder
    Shriek shuddering to the sea!

Through days that lagged as years yon sun hath
    sickened
  Behind foul fogs; its light made mock of light
Where spectral men crawled slow; where raw noon
    thickened
      To chill mist-clotted night:

Night where the stars were dead; where vapours
    blotted
  The mystic glamour from the ancient sky;
Where sodden fields lay dark with sheaves that
    rotted;
        Where sad men ceased to sigh!

But lo! this stalwart wind has blown, and harried
  The nightmare fog back to its grim, foul den;
While hardy joy, and timid hope that tarried,
        Dance in the hearts of men!

VISION

WHERE careless diggers dug their clay
  Was left a deep red pit;
Hard by men's daily path it lay,
  Yet none regarded it.

Betimes the heaven brimmed it bright
  With clear grey rain; its red
Waste heart grew quick; it throbbed with light;
  It lived that was so dead.

Within its ragged rim it held
  The sky's wide pomp; it drew
Sad beauty from the stars of eld;
  The last vain cloud it knew;

Quick morning brimmed it up with gold;
  The bannered noon blew there;
There twilight spread a crimson fold;
  Its fitful moons were fair.

Yet still no man regarded it
  Save one rapt soul; to him
The visions in that sombre pit
  Outshone the Cherubim.

He loved it well; at night and morn,
  Twilight, and lustered noon,
With heart elate, with heart forlorn,
  He went to crave its boon.

THE SPHINX IN ROTTEN ROW

THAT world has gone; that little world
Whose blazoned folly blows unfurled
Daily at four; the dazzled Row
Lies dim; the jewelled, jingling Show
Has shone its idle hour, and fares
Elsewhither with its perfumed cares!
But who is this perched on the fence
Who counts and clicks the greasy pence
From hand to hand; his crimson vest
Made wondrous by the crimsoned West?
All hail! thou peaceful organ-man,
Peace be with thee and all thy clan!
I know that feathered hat, those rings;
Thy shuffled gait not seldom brings

To me, alas! those worst of boons
Thy Tuscan smile, thy tawdry tunes!
But who is this perched on the pole,
This blinking, meditative Soul?
All hail! thou kinsman of the other,
His cousin, or at best, his brother,—
Albeit he binds thee in a chain
A hireling monkey for his gain!
Red is thy bonnet, and with red
Most bravely thou art jacketed;
Thine eyes are twitched in shine and shut,
While in thy cheek a cherished nut
Takes from the contour of thy face
Its haughty, pre-historic grace!
Grim prophecy of god-like man,
Sage when the elder world began,
What thoughts hast thou upon thy perch
With *men* beneath the nimble search
Of thy quick eyes?   O sad-faced fop,
Gay tumbler on this organ-top,
Seems all our Mighty Race to thee
Some foolishest fraternity

Of jigging apes; apes sent a-skip
To stale old tunes; our Earth a strip
Of grass-green baize whereon we strut
And dance (like thee) for some poor nut?
Mean exile! clowning it for alms,—
Thy Heaven a land of sunlit palms,—
Seems it to thee in this still Hour
That Man is slave to some dark Power
Who binds a thong about his middle;
Who grinds him music for a riddle,
Whereto he struts, with skip and hop,
Unwitting when the Tune shall stop?
O, blinking meditative Soul
Perched there upon the organ-pole,
With such deep questions dost thou task
Thy wit, behind that antique mask?
Nay, blink not; for thy simple blink
Prompts swift suspicion that thy wink
Is cynical; thy face were meek
Did not that nut clapt in thy cheek
Give to thy grin a vulgar guile
Unknown to pre-adamic smile!

Come, sly-faced Sphinx! let loose thy wit
And add thy gloss to what was writ
By Hebrew scribes; for thou must know
The genesis of Long Ago,—
The stark uprising of the Race
Who jingle here in joyless grace.
To find the time, the clime, the clan
Where Monkey slept and woke up Man,
Is our vain search; our wise are vext,
Our witlings mock the parson's text.
Out with thy tale, nor spare our pride,
Let wag thy wit whate'er betide;—
Whose was the mighty mind that rose
And snatched sublimity from clothes?
What dapper Monkey swift upgat
To gird his loins, to brush his hat,
That he, the first, might strut the glades
To dazzle anthropoidal maids?
O grey-faced Sphinx, let loose thy wit,
That so our braggart Race may sit
Beneath thy pole, and learn from thee
The world's primeval vanity!

Aha! thy face begins to wrinkle
And stir, as to some inward twinkle
Of age-old jest; thine eyes slow shut,
Thy face atwist—*crack goes the nut.*
'Od's life! the imp with chuckled glee
Tosses the empty shell at me!

BETROTHAL

THIS tale is old, this tale you have to tell;
   Sure many lips have told it; many eyes
   Shone to its telling under twilight skies,
Since thro' the splendour of the dusk there fell
The rich far-tinkle of a camel's bell,
   Swinging from Mesopotamia; dyes
   Deepen adown the West in weary-wise
Since Isaac met Rebecca by the well.

I sing amiss; thy tale, dear friend, is young;
   Forever young; old it makes all else seem;
   Nor dawn, nor spring-tide, nor the poet's dream
Starts with so fresh a grace, as when the tongue
   Loosens about its Love; filched of this theme
Earth had no tale her children could have sung.

MARRIAGE

HEART-FREEDOM is found, nor in praise nor in
  splendour
  When Bridegroom and Bride at the altar are
  bound;
But in vows which are true, as in loves which are
  tender,
        Heart-freedom is found:
As this song of my singing is woven and wound
  In a mesh of white rhyme, since haply its sender
Would marry his blessing to virgin-sweet sound,—
  So, love wears her bonds for the grace they shall
  lend her
To-day at the altar when two lives are crowned;
  For in depths of obedience and heights of sur-
  render
        Heart-freedom is found.

A POET PASSES

R. B., 12th December, 1889

LAST eve upon the lawn
  Heard we him sing
On topmost boughs withdrawn;
  Song with the old, high ring
  Heard we him sing.

Clear, though the West went wan,
  Clear went his song;
Winter had naught withdrawn;
  Rich, hopeful, joyous, strong,—
  Clear went his song.

But, when drew forth the dawn,
  Found we him dead;
To deeper skies withdrawn
  Singer and song had sped:
  Hush! he is dead.

MY CITY

Fresh winds afoot; white clouds afloat;
   The free sun fares on high;
These Cathkin Braes are glanced with light,
   Are gloomed where shadows fly;
While here alow, and there aloft
   The wild, shrill peesweeps cry.

Nor sun, nor clouds, nor flying shade,
   Nor aught of these I wist;
The piping wind, the peesweeps' cry,
   To naught of these I list;
For my heart is with yon city
   Grim-muffled in grey mist.

Yon city of Sanct Mungo; mine
  While heart within me beats;
Mine, when the tide of life drove high;
  Mine, now the tide retreats;
For I spilled my life like water,
  O city! in thy streets.

Not always did I love thee; yea,
  In youth a youth's despair
Rang curses where thy red nights burned
  Ghastly thro' sheeted glare;
Where great white stars reeled in sick fogs;
  Where sad men spectral were.

Not always did I curse thee; nay,
  In youth a youth's high hope,
Saw visions in thy thronging streets;
  Saw shining pathways ope
Thro' ragged smoke; saw leal, brave hearts
  Climb duty's laboured slope.

56

Love met me in thy midst; young Love
    Touched thy black streets to white;
Caught all thy clamoured tramplings
    And tuned them to delight;
For thy life throbbed bridal music—
    Bright as our loves were bright.

Death met me in thy midst; old Death
    Treads where thy toilers tread;
Jars through thy junkettings, and glooms
    Though bright flags burn o'erhead;
O city! through thy laughing streets
    I bore my silent dead.

Thus love and death, despair and hope,
    Have taught me what thou art!
Thy stormy life strikes deeper than
    The babble of the mart;
Not all of traffic is thy thought,
    Not all of stone thy heart.

H

O city of Sanct Mungo! mine
 While heart within me beats;
Mine, when the tide of life drove high;
 Mine, now the tide retreats;
For I spilled my life like water,
 O city! in thy streets.

PAX SINE PACE

Pause here: sure here is peace;
   Noon, and the drowse of noon;
   Waters in slumbrous tune;
Meadows with kine at ease;

Pools where clear waters flow,—
   Pools where the shining trout
   Flicker; while in and out,
Darkling their shadows go.

Smoothly the river slides
   Seaward; through tangled grass
   Swaying, its waters pass;
Blue at its heart abides.

Blue of the placid sky;
   Set in soft grace between
   Green banks, and shadowed green
The great depths of heaven lie.

Lo! from its silver lair
   Hunting the lazy fly,
   Gleaming a curve on high
Glances a trout in air:

Lo! from the blossomed thorn
   Swiftly on wings a-whirr
   Flashes the kingfisher;—
Straightway that trout is torn.

Peaceful the place, you say?
   Fool! it is red with strife;
   Ruthless, and swift, and rife,
Slayers come here to slay.

TO A NEW SCOTS AUTHOR!

SAUNDERS! you're young an' I am auld,
An' Age is blate where Youth is bauld;
But yet, afore ye leave the fauld
   To seek your fortin',
Here's twa-three words, baith het an' cauld,
   O' plain exhortin'.

Nae doot, my lad, in Lun'on toon
There's gowden plainstanes for your shoon;
Nae doot ilk kimmer wears a croon
   At kirk an' market;
Yet faith! I've kent an orra loon
   Slant hame half-sarkit!

61

Then wale your words, an' watch your stap,
An' keep a kist for ilka crap;
What though your wits are scant o' sap,
     That's safe between us;
Dour hirslin' tak's folk to the tap
     Quicker than gen'us!

That Brag grows fat when Blate gangs stervin'
Is God's ain truth in my observin';
Then praise yoursel' an' your deservin'
     Up hill, doon dale;
Let modest men for patient servin'
     Sup muslin-kail!

What though, in cadgin', curse an' cuff
Come at your lug wi' ettled buff;
Seek help frae Heaven when men are gruff
     An' damn your trog;—
But first seek them that write the puff
     An' rowe the log!

Sic chiels, I'm telt, noo rummage sair
To rout a gen'us frae his lair;
Lord man! put up a wee bit prayer
   That ane may catch ye;
For gif ye're catcht,—nine days an' mair
   There's nane shall match ye!

Heth! but the hill-taps then shall bleeze
Frae Fleet Street to the Hebrides!
Then honest men shall tell Diel's lees
   Withouten shame;
They'll puff your squint, they'll praise your sneeze
   To speed your fame!

Then, Saunders, lad, while Fortune ploos
Saw ye the seed; slip round the news
That you're at hame for interviews
   A' day, a' nicht;
Till at your door, in flocks like doos,
   The scrievers licht!

63

Welcome sic gentry,—cock an' hen;
Smiles for the maids, yill for the men;
Tak' them your hoose-place but an' ben,
            Wi' simple air;
Tell them the bonniest lees ye ken,—
            An' they'll tell mair!

Lord! but they'll deave the worl' wi' skirlin'
The bits o' clash yoursel' set birlin',
Till heaven an' John o' Groats are dirlin'
            As ne'er before;
Till publishers in droves come tirlin'
            At your ha'-door!

Then keep scrieve-scrievin' if you're wice,
Saft greetin' tales wi' sklents at Vice;
For Virtue comes an' gangs in price
            When Sin aye sells;
But mind ye, end your screeds wi' rice
            An' mairrage-bells!
64

Tak' this advice;—an' faith, ere Lammas
The Diel be fried! but ye'll be faamous;
Then gie a thocht to your frien' Tammas,
        The kindly-gruff;
An' send him North, by way of aumous,—
        Twa ounce o' snuff!

THROUGH A CHURCH WINDOW

WITHOUT the May sun shone; within
　　The preacher spun his shining text
With poor grey words; I heard him spin
　　His drowsy platitudes unvexed:
The gracious sunlight made me win
　　Praise for this world;—he praised the next.

Without I saw the dusk street shine
　　With soft Spring light; above the drone
Of future bliss came clear, divine
　　Laughter of little children; prone
To make all happy omens mine,
　　I knew man's world was still God's own.

For lo! these children fared, footsore,
    In ragged, laughing, straggling bands;
Back to the city's smoke they bore
    The hedgerow's blossom in their hands:
Such country wealth to them was more
    Than all the wealth of fabled lands.

I watched them pass; my eyes went dim
    With tears of some strange, high delight;
These children's lives were hard and grim,
    Yet earth had beauty in their sight;
They knew, these waifs, the ways of Him
    Who stars the thorn with red and white.

REVEILLE

THE birds are up, the buds are out,
  Winds free, and clouds aflit;
Sure he is but a dullard lout
Who lags abed with lambs about:
  God stir his cloddish wit.

Sad stint is his who hath not known
  The push of spring-time sap;
Whose life takes not the birds' high tone;
Whose love blows not when buds are blown:
  God mend his barren hap.

AFTERWARDS

RAN a child,—when skies went clear,
  When the rain had spent its might,
When the sun with laggard cheer
  Jewelled up the land with light,—

Ran a child with shining feet,
  Them to dabble in the flood,
Dancing down the village street,
  Quick with dead leaves, dark with mud.

When the merry tide had passed,
  Little pools of sudden dye
Gathered to their hearts the vast
  Vision of the evening sky.

When the child,—made still with awe
   By this glimpse of azure grace,—
Peered into a pool, he saw
   Heaven about a little face!

Home he went with loitered feet;
   Sought a silent place apart;
For to him the night was sweet,
   With this wonder in his heart.

Sad! the child with morning trust,
   Sought that pool of wondrous dye;
But he found a thin grey dust
   Where had shone a piece of sky.

MISUNDERSTOOD

I STOOD amid the tombs to-day,
   Where marble plinth and pillar rise;
Where Holy Writ gilds sordid clay;
   Where vice is tricked in virtue's guise.

And in a sodden place apart
   A very human word I found;
The story of a lonely heart,
   Set on a long-neglected mound.

A common mound of matted grass;
   A sunken cross rough-hewn in wood;
Whereon, amid the lichens, was
   The one brief word,—MISUNDERSTOOD.

Nor name, nor date was graven there;
  One word there was, and only one.
Enough! this nameless soul hath share
  With noblest names beneath the sun.

For what gives Earth of royal gift
  To all her starry sons who try
Through blame and bitterness to lift
  Light on man's life,—and fail,—and die?

Some common mound of matted weed;
  Some sunken cross rough-hewn in wood;
Whereon is set,—O bitter meed!—
  That one brief word,—MISUNDERSTOOD.

A GREEN VALLEY

IT was a quiet valley,
  Set far from human ills;
A sunny, sloping valley,
  Begirt with green, green hills.

The white clouds softly knitted
  Grey shadows in the grass;
The sea-birds poised and flitted,
  As they were loath to pass.

A clear stream thrid the bridges;
  Blue, lazy smoke upcurled;
Beyond the purple ridges
  Lay the unquiet world.

Under the ivied rafters
  Low-crooned the sun-drowsed dove;
While youthful, breezy laughters
  Moved on the slopes above,—

Where 'mid the flower-pied spaces,
  We children made bright quest;
Sure, as we ran quick races,
  The far-seen flower was best.

Fair shines that sunny valley,
  Set far from human ills;
Our childhoods' simple valley,
  Begirt with green, green hills.

CLOUDLAND

Fresh is the wind in its blowing,
  Over the spring-tide blue;
High are the clouds in their going,
  Afret where the winds pursue;
With beauty their only showing;
  White as with young content;
Gaily they go; without knowing
  Whence come, or whither sent.

From southward to westward drifted
  All of an April day;
Full lightly they swing, uplifted
  Over the city's grey;
Tossed free of the wind, and rifted
  In gaps of sudden blue;
Caught warm of the sun, and sifted
  With clear light through and through.

O'er shadowless deeps of azure,
  All as the wise winds blow,
With a seemly grace of leisure,
  Cloud after cloud they go;
In a dance of sunny pleasure
  That keepeth high and clear,
As unto an airy measure,
  Too fine for human ear.

I watch them drift and dally,
  And shine as they were wet,
With the clear light blown in sally
  Of winds that veer and fret:—
Till my youth-dreams rise, and rally,
  And press me still to seek
Yon Cloudland of slope and valley
  Sun-touched on one pure peak.

WANDERERS

SAT we there in the noon together,
  Laid in spell by the clouds on high;
Sat in the sun and dreamed together,
Drowsed and dreamed in the still white weather,
  My soul, my shadow, and I.

Far we fared in the morn together,
  Lured of hopes that haunt the sky;
Far thro' the gleams of the magic weather,
Forth in a band we fared together,
  My soul, my shadow, and I.

77

Much we met in the morning weather;
  Creeds that fail and Lights that die;
No two things that chime together
Met we there in the rosy weather,
  My soul, my shadow, and I.

Thus we sat in the noon together,
  Sat and watched the clouds go by;
Naught to us was the still white weather:—
We were alone in the land together,
  My soul, my shadow, and I.

A TRAGIC WORD

ATHWART the whistling ice we wheeled
Through that white day; the blanched hills reeled;
The blue above rang like a shield:

A day of fierce delight.   At last
My woman's whim a chance word cast;
A light word,—and you gloomed and passed.

Your quick heel crunched across the snow;
I watched to see you turn; but no,
Your skate-blades clashed: you left me so.

A dreary throstle chirped,—" Wait, wait ";
With proud heart rocked by Love and Hate,
Wretched, I waited at the gate.

The white moon clomb above the height
Through ragged pines; she mocked my plight,
That virgin moon who ruled the night.

The stern owls hooted; well they knew
That love, by waiting, comes to few;—
And never sign has come from you.

AN OLD SONG

WHERE sunlight sets its latticed gleams
   On oaken walls adance,
There Doris sits; there Doris dreams
   Of mirth and old romance.

For while she plies the spinet's keys
   And hums an ancient song,
She sees, through ruddy lights she sees
   The hall with guests athrong.

She hears the viol's tender note
   Lead forth the trembling flute,
To set with grace the light gavotte
   For dancers blythe of foot.

          L

Nor wots the maid that earth is boon
  With songs as bright to-day;—
'Tis still for youth a wistful tune
  That once the world was gay.

So Doris dreams that bliss befell
  When this old song was new;
Ah! round these walls grim faces tell
  How mirth was worn with rue.

IN THE NIGHT SEASON

THOU art with me, O Beloved,
   Thou art with me in the night,—
When the dark is at the deepest
   When sleep gifts the soul with sight,—
Thou art with me, O Beloved,
   In a dream of old delight.

In a glimpse of still spring weather
   With the sunlight on thy head,
Thou art waiting, O Beloved,
   Thou art waiting who wast dead;
And our lips go warm together
   As it was when we were wed.

Yea, we greet with fair good-morrow
  All untouched of Earth's surprise,
As we pass into the meadow
  Where the simple sunshine lies;
Yea, no shade of all our sorrow
  Dims the shining of thine eyes.

Down the path we wander slowly,
  Down the path we went of old,
By the river's sunlit shallow
  Where it sings o'er lambent gold;
And the place to us is holy
  For the love that here was told.

Dear! it seems we have not parted
  Where the ways forever cease;
All the years before us brighten
  With a love that shall increase;
Dear! I am not lonely-hearted,
  And thy face is fair with peace.

Nay, our hearts have no misgiving
  While the sweet dream holds its sway;
But Beloved, O Beloved!
  At the dawning of the day
I am lone among the living,
  Thou art Dream for aye and aye!

THE NOR'LAND SEA

OH! sea of my youth thy spell is strong
  To weave me many a shining thought;
The mystic trouble that stirs in song
  Takes motion when thy spell is wrought:
As a stranger here unloved, unknown,
As I walk these grey-grim streets alone,
  From far away in the North Countree
  Comes many a haunting lilt to me
    From the old Nor'land Sea.

A waste grey sea and a wide grey sky;
  Salt wind from the eastward keenly set;
The white gulls sweeping afar and anigh;
  An old man mending an old brown net;
A child at play by the open door;
A voice that shall sound for me no more;—
  Oh! faint and afar though these things be
  They live with the love that beat for me
    By the old Nor'land Sea.

As a cradle-croon it set, meseems,
  This heart astir with its ancient strife;
It lapped me asleep and led my dreams
  In the dim unlaboured dawn of life;
For the laughing boy it kept a tune,
For the dreaming youth an unread rune;
  And still its melody follows free,
  To keep it soothfast and fond in me,
    This old-loved Nor'land Sea.

In the summer noon it held me slave
  With sun-bright music brave and strong;
In depths of a windy wave-plashed cave
  It touched me a weird unworded song;
When the stars beat up the breezeless lift,
When the moon sent tangled light adrift,
  When the mystic sails passed slow to lee
  Came many a way-lost lilt to me
    From the wide Nor'land Sea.

Oh! sea of my youth, thy life is here
  Where now my wandering feet abide;
Yea, I hear thy loud note ringing clear
  In this Southland city's human tide;
In an ebb and flow of thunder-tones
That beat forever along its stones;
  In its brooding gulfs that sunless be,
  In its unhushed sobbing it tells of thee,
    Thou restless Nor'land Sea.

I wander unhailed along these streets,
   My heart all heavy with thoughts of home;
I watch *this* tide as it beats and beats,
   With its sodden fringe of salt, salt foam;
Yet though these waters be grey and sad
They stir the soul of this stranger-lad;
   In this mystic-waved humanity
   I catch the music that set for me
      Across the Nor'land Sea.

MY HILLS

Thou art weary, my Heart, I know, I know;
And I list thee telling in whispers low,
That life would be sweeter where Spring winds
blow
About the hills.

For this city's mirth is a madman's glee,
And its wanton music a dirge to thee;
Thou wert thrilled with ethereal melody
Among the hills.

Thou art dreaming, my Heart, of bright days, when
We wandered far from the ways of men;
Thou art haunted with silence from yon green glen
Girt by the hills;

90

Where the gold-fretted peaks foretell the day;
Where white clouds hover, where cool shadows
    play;
Where the pale stars glint in the mystic grey
        Beyond the hills.

Thou art lonely, my Heart, in this city's throng;
Dumb in its clamour, all sad with its wrong;
But thine is the fellowship free and strong
        Of the old hills.

They are kin with thee in a chequered life;
With quick-gleaming lights, with dark shadows
    rife;
Babes of one Mother, birth-bound in one strife,
        Thou and the hills.

O, hush thee, my Heart! for thy wailing seems
Fed with the music of dark-sobbing streams,
That moan to the stars in their restless dreams
        'Mid the lone hills.

O, hush thee! but keep this glad thought in my
    breast,
To lighten the burden, to give toil a zest,—
That in life is peace, and with death is rest
        Beyond the hills.

TO ARMS!

GIRD thee for warfare, O my soul!
    Nor brood on creeds that bruised thy life;
The only salve shall make thee whole,
    Is greater daring, direr strife.

Be thou no bondsman to the Past;
    Nor yield the tyrant Future sway;
`Bring to this warfare what thou hast,
    And stand for all thy strength, To-day.

Let old fights go; this day is thine;
    Yon sun is for a freeman's need;
Naught but the dawnless Dark is sign
    That earth can do without thy deed.

FROM DIOGENES; GREETING

POETS, this chaunt for you!
Great was your art to set men's hearts aglow
With visioned promise of what men might know
Of fair, wise, true; to rouse races to march
That else were chained; to fling a fearless arch
Of friendly song from land to land; to light
The great blind centuries thro' utmost night
With hill-top chaunts of dawn.   Thrice great your
    art
When fierce-tongued singers of the tender-heart
Made harps of prison-bars; when leapt their notes
Like sudden steel athwart all tyrant throats;
When song smacked of Mount Sinai;—such the
    power
These ancients had.   How is it at this hour?
Long have I looked, O dainty Poets, yea
Loud have I prayed (as in this tub I may)
That some uncouth, wild, prophet-voice would rise
Chaunting an iron song; a bard mad-wise,

Whose cry would shrill across your jingling, sweet
Trills, like cannon-music to victorious feet
Trampling where nautch-girls danced; a radiant
    bard
Whose songs were light though heaven were all
    unstarred!
Yet comes he not! Come still your motley throng
Thrumming on banjos; ballade, sonnet, song
Spin to the crowd agape, as jugglers spin
Their gilded balls; your praise the public grin!
Are all the tyrants dead? are all men free
That Poesy goes jigging thus? has She
Whose glory made the mighty Masters blench
Become, to-day, each strolling mummer's wench
Dancing to lightest tunes?   Answer me true.
        Poets, I chaunt for you!

www.ingramcontent.com/pod-product-compliance
Lightning Source LLC
Chambersburg PA
CBHW020041030726
47499CB00007B/2522